FREE SP Guidebook

Kerry Burki

Copyright © 2019 by Kerry Burki
All rights reserved. This book or any portion thereof
may not be reproduced or used in any manner whatsoever
without the express written permission of the publisher
except for the use of brief quotations in a book review.

Printed in the United States of America

ISBN 9781691874873

hello@kerryburki.com
www.KerryBurki.com

DEDICATION

This book is dedicated to all free spirits, including my two boys, Simon and Isaak. You are made of stars. I love you so much. If you ever feel lost or alone, I hope you have tools that guide you back to your heart. Your smiles have always done that for me.

SPECIAL THANKS

To my mom, thank you for always being by my side and supporting my free spirit ways. Thank you for loving me during the times when I wasn't so lovable. You always see my best self. For that, along with your constant support, I am forever grateful.

To Matt, you're my soul mate. When you look at me, you see my true beauty on a deep level. You make me laugh when I get too serious, point me in the right direction when I get turned around, and love me fiercely. We are so lucky. I love you, babe. Forever and ever.

IN GRATITUDE

God, Angels, Bear, Gloria, Nana Madeline, Wolf, Hummingbirds, Big Cats, Elephant, Buffalo, and all my guides, thank you for always being by my side. I am grateful for your presence and your guidance. Thank you for helping me create this guidebook and share it with the world.

ART LOVE

The beautiful dreamcatchers you see throughout this guidebook are painted by my color-dripping, free spirit, soul sister, Kristen Fagan of Kristen Fagan Art and Design. All other designs were either created or edited by me, Kerry Burki, or found under the Creative Commons CC0 or Public Domain Photos or purchased with a Commercial Use Extended License. Thank you to all the creative souls for helping make this guidebook so beautiful!

CONTENTS

Introduction

Part 1: Working with Nature   6
Working with Crystals   9
Flower Clearing Exercise   16
Candle Gazing   19
Decluttering is Magic   22
Clearing Your Space with Smoke and Sound   25
Working with Essential Oils   31
Change Your Posture, Change Your Life   36

Part 2: Working with your Breath   39
Connecting the Sun, the Moon, and your Breath   42
Releasing Breath   45
Meeting Challenges with Victory Breath   48
Breath of Fire   51
Alternate Nostril Breathing   54

Part 3: Working with your Thoughts   57
Check In   60
Have Fun & Draw In   61
More or Less   64
Letter to Younger Self   67
Thoughts Become Things   70
I AM Meditation   73
Dream Big   76

Part 4: Working with your Imagination and Energy   79
Get Grounded   82
Tap into your Intuition   85
Working with Animal Guides   89
Working with your Runners   98
Color Energy   101
Naming Your Higher Self   105
Working with Angels   108
Clearing Visualization   111
Protection Visualization   115
Knowing your Chakras   118
Living by the Light of the Moon   123

Moving Forward and Bonuses   129

INTRODUCTION

Are you ready to be a free spirit? Maybe you already are one. Either way, this guidebook will help you get grounded in your personal energy and what it means to you to be a free spirit.

The idea of being a free spirit is often associated with going against social norms. That is why I chose it as the title for this guidebook. The lessons here are not what everyone is doing every day or what you regularly see in the media.

Right off the bat, you will have to be open-minded. Allow the work in this guidebook to reveal parts of yourself that you have been searching for.

It will take courage and discipline. Often, words like discipline and structure are not words that are associated with being a free spirit. However, when you set aside time to tend to yourself regularly, you will begin to experience a level of freedom that you have never felt before.

Free spirits are known for their independence, and this guide will help you march to the beat of your own drum.

Whether you are a homebody or world traveler, the lessons in this guidebook will help you feel grounded and connected wherever you are. Get ready to embrace your journey to free spirit living! This guide is filled with simple ways to help you start enjoying life more.

It is a mix of my creations, ancient techniques from my yogic studies, tried and true life coaching exercises, along with energy work from my experience as a metaphysical teacher and intuitive counselor.

I am not going to teach you how to live my way, however. Everything I share will help you become a more authentic version of yourself. You will be drawn to different lessons and begin to use them in your unique way in your life.

You will learn how to empower yourself and shift your energy to a higher vibration.

If you commit to working on the tips and exercises, you will feel a massive positive shift in the flow and experience of your life.

This work will help you feel more like yourself and more confident in the choices you make. I am not saying you won't have bad days.

The goal of the work I am sharing is to help you learn how to handle the ups and downs of life with more grace and ease.

You will learn how to tune out the world around you and tune into your inner wisdom. You will have resources to change your mood, your thoughts, your breath, and your life.

Your life might change, or you might change how you look at your life. Or both! Either way, you will feel empowered by the work you do and happy that you have committed to bringing positive change into your life.

Take a moment and thank yourself for taking this time for yourself.

You might want to create a special place in which to do the work in this guide. This space could be a room, a chair, a nook. Maybe just a basket or tray that will contain the tools you want around you as you work through this guide.

Doing this will help you transition from your day to taking this special time for yourself. It will become a sacred space for you. You might like to have candles, matches, incense, essential oils, etc. Make it yours.

You might like to get a special journal to write down your reflections and responses or use the printable worksheets I created for you by visiting www.kerryburki.com/free-spirit-bonuses.

There is a positive affirmation at the end of each lesson that you might like to incorporate into your life or possibly repeat when you are practicing the lessons.

There is a lot of information in this guide, and I want to let you know that you will not be incorporating all of it into your daily life. Instead, think of it as a toolbox you can use to help you get unstuck, pumped up, relaxed, goal-oriented, and so on.

When you are first starting, you might like to keep your efforts private. Honor your feelings around how you share the time you take for yourself.

You will have different needs at different times, and this guide will feel like a comforting space to come back to help you tune in and remember who you really are.

Get ready, free spirit! I hope you enjoy this journey!

xo, Kerry

Part 1:

WORKING WITH *Nature*

TOOLS AND TECHNIQUES THAT USE THE PHYSICAL WORLD TO HELP RELEASE STRESS AND COPE WITH LIFE SO YOU CAN RELAX AND BE HAPPY.

"Every particular in nature, a leaf, a drop, a crystal, a moment of time is related to the whole, and partakes of the perfection of the whole."
– Ralph Waldo Emerson

WORKING WITH *Nature*

In Part 1, you will be working with elements from nature such as crystals, plants, and your own body.

Taking time for yourself and working with tangible items is a great way to begin to notice the power you have in your own life. These lessons require an open mind and, for the most part, they all include immediate results which are the perfect way to start this journey.

By the end of this section, you will be using crystals and essential oils regularly. You will have at least one area of your home decluttered. You will have spent some time meditating with a candle, using a flower (or a vision of a flower), smoke, and sound to clear away worries and negative energy, and lastly, you will be standing taller.

Lessons:
- Working with Crystals
- Flower Clearing Exercise
- Candle Gazing
- Decluttering is Magic!
- Clearing Your Space with Smoke and Sound
- Working with Essential Oils
- Change Your Posture, Change Your Life

"You are drawn to the one you need."
— Azalea Lee

WORKING WITH Crystals

If you are like me, you have been collecting crystals and stones for years. What started as a hobby of collecting pretty ones quickly turned into a self-care and manifesting extravaganza!

Crystals and stones have qualities associated with them that you can use for healing.

Two ways to pick crystals and stones:
 1. Look up the qualities associated first and then get the ones that appeal to you.
 2. Look at stones and choose the ones that appeal to you, then look up the qualities.

After this, the real magic happens. You will find a list of common and popular crystals on the following pages. Before you do any of the recommended rituals with your chosen stone, you will want to cleanse it and then empower it with your intentions.

You can cleanse your stones by holding them in the sacred smoke from a smudge stick or incense. You can also place them in moonlight, sunlight, salt, dirt, or water for 1 hour to 24 hours. Water, salt, and sunlight are not recommended for some stones so be sure to do a little research first or simply stick with the other methods.

You can cleanse when they are new, when you want to work more closely with one, during certain moon phases, or simply after a bit of time has passed without cleansing them.

When you are cleansing them, do it with the intention of getting rid of any old or stagnant energy attached to the stone and imagine it being cleared and ready for your intentions when you are done.

WORKING WITH *Crystals*

After you have cleansed your crystals, you can empower them with your intentions. These intentions can be based on the characteristics of the crystal or your intention.

Hold your stone in your hand and envision your crystal being filled with bright light. It might be white light or a color associated with the crystal.

Close your eyes and whisper your intention. Example: If you are going to be carrying Smoky Quartz around with you to keep you grounded, you would hold it in your hand and say any variation of the following:

- I intend to stay grounded while in the presence of this crystal.
- Thank you for keeping me grounded when you are by my side.
- I empower you to keep me grounded and connected to earth energy.

You could also put it in the form of a request or prayer:

- What are some ways I can stay grounded today?
- Please allow the energy from this stone to keep me grounded.

Then go on to use the stone as recommended or create a new way to incorporate it into your life.

You can use different stones during different phases of the moon, dedicate one to your New Moon Intention, place them in various areas of your home, pick a few that have the energy you need right now and carry them with you.

The possibilities are endless, so have fun!

WORKING WITH Crystals

GREEN AVENTURINE

Known as the Stone of Opportunity. Associated with luck and success.

Chakra: Heart

- Carry it in your left pocket as a lucky charm.
- Wear it as jewelry for prosperity and protection.

SODALITE

Known as the Poet's Stone or Harmony Stone.

Chakra: Throat and Brow

- Place it on your throat or third-eye to help calm your words or thoughts.
- Keep it near when writing or trying to connect with your intuition.

HOWLITE

Known as the Stone of Reasoning and Discernment.

Chakra: Crown

- Carry it with you when you feel called to act tactfully in a situation.
- Wear as jewelry for a calming and soothing energy.

RED JASPER

Known for is grounding and stabilizing properties. It also helps with anxiety.

Chakra: Root

- Hold while doing a grounding meditation.
- Carry it with you to help stabilize your mood throughout the day.

SNOWFLAKE OBSIDIAN

Known for its grounding and protective qualities.

Chakra: Root

- Hold in in your hand for a quick release of anger.
- Add it to a protective charm bag that you carry with you or place it in a special area in your home.

RAINBOW FLUORITE

Known as the Wise Sage Stone. Helps with focus and calm.

Chakra: Heart, Throat, Third-Eye (Brow), and Crown

- Keep it in meditation space to help cleanse your aura.
- Gaze at the colors as a ritual to help your mind relax or place under your pillow when feeling stressed.

WORKING WITH Crystals

CARNELIAN

Known as a Feel Better Stone.

Chakra: Sacral

- Keep near for energy with creative endeavors.
- Place on your sacral chakra to help balance sexual energy.

CITRINE

Known as the Money Stone. Enhances optimism and energy.

Chakra: Solar Plexus

- Place in wallet or purse for abundance.
- Carry it with you when you need a little pick-me-up.

MOONSTONE

Known for its soothing, cooling, feminine energy.

Chakra: Sacral, Heart, Third-Eye (Brow) and Crown

- Place stones around for a happy home.
- Carry with you to remind you to find your natural rhythm like the phases of the moon.

SMOKY QUARTZ

Known for its grounding and protective properties.

Chakra: Root

- Carry with you to keep you feeling grounded or in your workspace for focus.
- Hold it in your hand and allow it to absorb and transmute any of the negativity you are carrying.

ANGELITE

Known as a soothing and calming stone that facilitates healing.

Chakra: Throat and Crown

- Place it on an altar to help you connect with your angels.
- Place it under your pillow to encourage peaceful sleep.

CLEAR QUARTZ

Enhances clarity and spiritual connection.

Chakra: All

- Place it near other crystals to amplify their energy.
- Empower it with an intention and carry it with you, place it in a special place, or put it on your altar.

WORKING WITH Crystals

AMETHYST

Enhances connection to the divine, spirituality, awareness, and imagination.

Chakra: Crown

- Place in main living area to create a calm yet uplifting atmosphere.
- Put under your pillow or on your nightstand to help strengthen your connection to the divine.

TIGER'S EYE

Encourages optimism. Known to help you feel grounded during times of stress. Connects you with your gut instincts and personal power.

Chakra: Solar

- Carry in your pocket or purse when you need to feel confident.
- Gaze at the stone as a way to bring you into the present moment.

SELENITE

Transmutes negative energy into positive or neutral energy. Associated with the Moon.

Chakra: Crown

- Use it as a wand to clear the space around you.
- Place with tarot or oracle cards to keep them cleansed from other people's energy.

ROSE QUARTZ

Enhances romantic love, self-love, and universal love.

Chakra: Heart

- Carry this stone to help heal heartbreak and encourage self-love.
- Display this stone in the center (heart) of your home to promote a loving environment.

TURQUOISE

Enhances creative expression, clear communication, and connection to your personal truth.

Chakra: Throat

- Place a piece on your throat during a reclined meditation to help you speak your truth.
- Wear as jewelry to remind you of your inner wisdom.

BLACK TOURMALINE

Known as a protection stone and energy purifier.

Chakra: All

- Wear or carry this when you know you are going to be around people or in situations that drain your energy.
- Place it on each chakra to help clear that chakra.

I empower my crystals with my intentions and create a life I love.

"She wore flowers in her hair & carried magic secrets in her eyes."
— Arundhati Roy

Flower
CLEARING EXERCISE

Flowers have been associated with beauty, health, and magic for a very long time. I learned this technique while I was in college, and it is one of my favorites. Plus, you can play around with it and truly make it your own.

When you are feeling crabby, tired, or frustrated, sometimes it is because you have been picking up other people's energy all day long.

This simple and fun exercise is a beautiful way to consciously clear your energetic space (aura) so you can get back in touch with your feelings and energy.

Imagine you are holding a beautiful flower by the stem in your hand. Slowly start to move the flower all around your body. Imagine negative energy that you have picked up sticking to the petals. Flick the flower away from you to disperse that energy and imagine it disappearing or turning into positive or neutral energy. Move around your whole body until you feel a bit lighter and clearer.

Try doing the physical the movements while holding an imaginary or real flower. Take notice of the flower that you chose. Work with it often or have fun doing this with different flowers. Consider looking up the meanings behind flowers to find out if they have any messages for you. You might also like to bring this flower into your life as a flower, candle, perfume, art, etc.

Also, remember that you can do this clearing in your mind in a pinch too. Maybe after leaving a particularly toxic meeting or when you are tired at the end of your day. Imagine your flower magically moving around your body and clearing away the negative energy you have accumulated. When you are finished, imagine yourself being filled with and surrounded by bright white light.

I am connected to flowers and their energy clears my aura.

"Man loves company – even if it is only that of a small burning candle."
– Georg C. Lichtenberg

Candle Gazing

Candle Gazing is an ancient yogic technique that is also called steady gazing or tratak. This technique helps lessen the feelings of separation and induces feelings of oneness with the universe.

Choose a candle and place it where the flame will be about eye level and arms distance away. Once the candle is lit, you will gaze at the flame for one minute. Use a timer.

After the minute is over, you will close your eyes and imagine the flame right between your eyebrows at your Third-eye Center (Brow Chakra). Using a timer, you can do this for two minutes.

To finish, cup your eyes with your hands for a moment. Then blow the candle out.

You can work up to more minutes or watch the whole candle burn or just do this for as long as it feels right for you that day.

Be sure to be comfortable by sitting in a chair or a comfortable seated meditation position.

It is okay if you blink at first. It takes practice to be able to keep your eyes open the whole time. Also, the ability to do so will fluctuate depending on the situations in your life.

Your eyes will water, and that helps to cleanse them and the tear ducts. This technique helps strengthen your eyes and boosts concentration and memory.

I like using this technique when I have no energy.
It is a perfect substitution for meditation.

It is also very calming.

Allow it to be a soothing addition to your self-care routine.

"The first step in crafting the life you want is to get rid of everything you don't."
— Joshua Becker

DECLUTTERING IS *Magic!*

Decluttering can change your life! Engaging in decluttering as a self-care and spiritual practice can help with anxiety, feelings of overwhelm, and spending too much time waiting for things to happen. The bonus is that things get decluttered!

This simple action is just the ticket to help you take your mind off meddling thoughts and take charge of an area of your life that needs more positive energy. It works like a charm.

You feel good about yourself after. You feel like you accomplished something which helps you shift to feeling more confident and happy. These positive feelings are what help you draw in more of what you want in your life.

Decluttering is the act of removing unnecessary items, possibly from an untidy or overcrowded space. One way to decide if something is clutter is to look at the item and ask yourself if it gives you energy or drains your energy.

With this in mind, pick an area to declutter like:

- kitchen
- drawer
- garage
- closet
- car
- purse
- nightstand
- desk

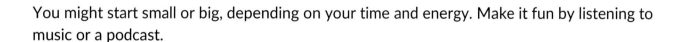

You might start small or big, depending on your time and energy. Make it fun by listening to music or a podcast.

Set an intention when you begin. Something like: I release things that take energy from me with joy and ease. You might like to repeat this while you declutter also.

Notice how you feel after. Consider doing a small amount of decluttering each week or when you are feeling stuck, lost, overwhelmed, anxious, or out of control.

Use the act of decluttering like a magic wand that can take you from feeling "blah" to "yah!"

I release things that take energy from me with joy and ease.

"Having a clear mind and a clear space allows you to think and act with purpose."
— Erika Oppenheimer

CLEARING YOUR SPACE WITH
Smoke & Sound

Clearing yourself and your space with smoke and sound has been done in different cultures for centuries.

Both are empowering ways to rid yourself and your space of negative or stagnant energy. This could be energy that was recently picked up, or that has been lingering for years. Think of it as energy that is not serving you or is no longer serving you.

While you are clearing, you can imagine that the negative or stagnant energy is being transmuted into neutral energy or clear space.

Spaces to clear:
- space around you (your aura)
- your home
- specific rooms
- entryways
- your car
- furniture
- items such as books and accessories

The list could go on and on!

Create an intention for this work.
"Help me clear this space from old, stagnant energy."
"Any energy here that is keeping me stuck is being cleared."
"With my intention and this smoke (or sound), I clear this space of any negative energy."

You can clear your space before doing spiritual work, before working with others, and after people have been over. You can also clear it if it has been a while since you last cleared your space, when you move into a new space, after negative or traumatic events have happened, every waning moon, or simply when you feel like it.

With my intention and this sound, I clear this space of any negative energy.

"Energy may be invisible to most of us, but that doesn't mean it isn't there!"
— Tess Whitehurst

CLEARING YOUR SPACE WITH
Smoke & Sound

With sound, you can imagine the sound reverberating around and into all of the nooks and crannies of your space shaking up and clearing negative or stagnant energy.

With smoke, you can allow it to burn in one spot or move around bringing the smoke into different spaces.

Always be very careful with lit embers and ashes. You might like to use an incense holder, seashell, or similar object to catch ashes. You can also put incense in a pot or jar with sand and stick in there. Be mindful to put out your smoke after you are done clearing or allowing it to burn out with supervision.

Allow both sound and smoke to go into areas around our body, under chairs, under your bed, in corners, nooks and crannies, and so on.

Here are some common tools you can use to clear space.
- smudge bundles - sage, mugwort, cedarwood, juniper
- palo santo
- incense
- singing bowls
- hand drums
- chimes
- hands (clapping)

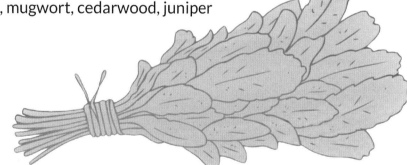

If you are new to this type of work, play around with what types of smoke and sound that you like best to get you started. If you are not new to this work, challenge yourself to find a new sound or smoke to bring into your routine.

After, protect and bless the space by imagining white light filling the space or a bubble or angels around the space or spritzing with rosewater or placing crystals around.

With my intention and this smoke, I clear this space of any negative energy.

KEEP CALM AND APPLY ESSENTIAL OILS.

WORKING WITH
Essential Oils

Are you obsessed with essential oils? If not, you might be after this lesson.

Once you find out the ones that ground you, give you energy, shift your focus, and so on, you will LOVE having them be a part of your everyday life.

Essential oils come from plants and are associated with the healing power of the plant.

Two ways to pick essential oils to work with:
  1. Look up the qualities first and then get the ones you need right now.
  2. Smell the oils first, pick the ones you are drawn to, then look up the qualities.

Many health food stores now carry essential oils, and this is the perfect place to start. You might also have a friend who is a representative of an oil company. If they host an event, you can go and sample the oils and learn more about your favorites.

Stay open to what you discover.

I ordered Cedarwood to put in a bug spray and discovered it is one of my favorite smells EVER.

Then I found out that it helps people feel grounded, which is exactly how it makes me feel. I don't even use the actual oil that much, I like to hold the bottle and inhale deeply.

The funny thing is, no one else in my family likes Cedarwood. So it would not be their choice when they want to feel more grounded. That is precisely why I encourage you to play around with the oils.

You might find that you like to use different ones throughout your day or that you just get hooked on one for a while. Allow the healing power of plants to work their mojo in your life!

WORKING WITH
Essential Oils

On the following page are a few popular essential oils. I have included simple ways to use them in your daily life.

Inhale - This is the simplest way to use essential oils. You can make a bottle last so long by simply inhaling the scent. You might like to carry a bottle in your bag, keep one at your desk, have one on your nightstand, etc. Doing this will help you to use them and reap the benefits with ease.

Apply topically - Most oils can be applied to the body. Everybody is different. Citrus essential oils are photosensitive so it is best not to put them on skin that will be exposed to sunlight. It is also recommended to use a carrier oil to dilute the oils. This is especially true for those with sensitive skin. Carrier oils can be grapeseed oil, jojoba oil, avocado oil, and sweet almond oil.

Diffuse - Adding essential oils to water in a diffuser can help spread the scent and healing properties of the oil into a larger space.

Spray - Another popular use is adding essential oils to a glass spray bottle with water. You can also add a small bit of vodka or witch hazel to help disperse the oils. The size of the bottle and the strength of the scent you desire will determine how many drops to add. Start with about 10 drops and increase until you are satisfied.

Bath - You can add a few drops to your bath to help you enjoy the scent as you relax and rejuvenate.

Use the descriptions on the following page plus your experiences with each scent to help you create rituals in your life that can be healing, help with daily life, and also create quality time with family members like a foot massage.

WORKING WITH Essential Oils

LAVENDER

- 2 drops on wrists twice a day to release tension.
- Temples and back of neck for stress.
- Bottoms of feet to promote a sense of calm.
- Diffuse or rub behind ears at bedtime.
- Inhale or diffuse before Savasana at the end of yoga practice.

PEPPERMINT

- Inhale for improved energy.
- Spritz with water or inhale to improve concentration for kids (and adults).
- Apply to forehead and temples for headaches.
- Mix with Lavender and water for a cooling spray.
- Rub on tummy to help with digestion.

LEMON

- When using on the body, always use a carrier oil such as jojoba, sweet almond, or avocado.
- Rub on bottoms of feet to help detox the liver.
- Diffuse to lift your mood.
- Inhale every morning to help you wake up.
- Rub on tummy to help with digestion.

PATCHOULI

- Apply to wrists, neck, or behind the ears as a perfume.
- Diffuse during a massage, yoga, or meditation for a calming effect.
- Diffuse after work or school to create a relaxing environment.
- Inhale as a natural anti-depressant.
- Rub it on neck or bottoms of feet at bedtime to help with insomnia.

FRANKINCENSE

- Inhale to reduce stress.
- Use in prayer or meditation to elevate your experience.
- Add to bath.
- Diffuse during yoga or self-massage.
- Blend with Lemon for a pick me up.
- Blend with Lavender as a relaxant.

CEDARWOOD

- Rub above eyebrows to release tension.
- Inhale or diffuse for a grounding effect.
- Apply to sides and back of head at bedtime to help let go of a bad habit.
- Inhale a few times a day to improve focus in kids (and adults).

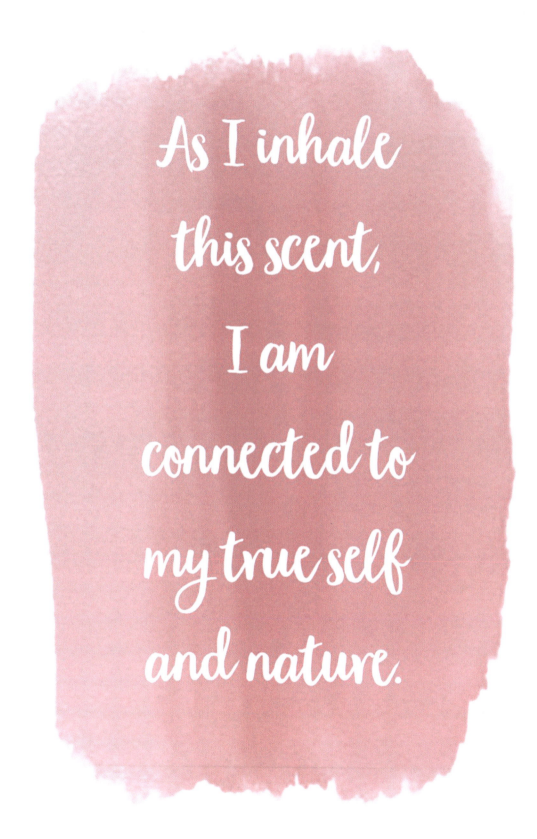

As I inhale this scent, I am connected to my true self and nature.

"Stand up straight and realize who you are, that you tower over your circumstances." – Maya Angelou

CHANGE YOUR Posture CHANGE YOUR LIFE

Do you have good posture or poor posture? When it comes to manifesting what we want in our lives, good posture can help. Think about it, so often we are hunched over and not feeling open to the possibilities around us.

Posture and energy flow are connected. When we have poor posture, it blocks the flow of energy. This negatively affects us on a mental, physical, and spiritual level.

We don't usually feel that great about ourselves when we are slumped a lot. Try it right now. Go from slumping to sitting or standing straight. Notice how your attitude experienced a shift, even if it was a small one.

Slumping closes you off from taking deeper breaths, sharing your heart, and receiving abundance.

This is a subtle shift that can help you literally open up to all of the good that wants to come your way.

Pay attention to your posture. Get in the habit of checking in and correcting your posture. Pay attention to the positive shift you feel each time.

If you are particularly tight or stiff, then do some shoulder and neck rolls. Also, give those areas some self-massage.

Notice other people's posture this week. Pay attention to the energy they are giving off. Think about the energy you want to give off and allow your posture to reflect that. Have fun!

(This page is dedicated to my Dad. Thank you for always correcting my posture. XO!)

As I improve my posture, I improve my life.

Part 2:

WORKING WITH YOUR Breath

BREATHING EXERCISES THAT WILL HELP YOU SHIFT YOUR ENERGY IN POSITIVE WAYS WHILE BRINGING HEALTH BENEFITS TO YOUR BODY AND MIND.

When you own your breath, nobody can steal your peace.

Working with your Breath

In Part 2, you will be working with your breath. In yoga, the regulation of the breath through specific techniques and exercises is called pranayama. If you are new to breathing exercises or would like to follow some videos, you might want to visit my blog at www.kerryburki.com/blog/.

Learning to use breathing techniques is a quick way to create and experience a positive shift in your life. Your body has many treasures to offer you. These lessons will help you tap into them while experiencing numerous benefits.

By the end of this section, you will know how to use your breath to calm, energize, release negative or old energy, bring about success, bust out of a bad mood, and balance your mind. You will also know how to use your breath to connect with the energy of the sun and moon.

***Do not practice these breaths in the same sitting. Working through this section will be a little different. You can try them throughout the day and possibly throughout the week when you are first starting. Then you can use then based on your situation going forward.

***If you have health conditions, you should consult with your doctor.

Lessons:
- Connecting the Sun, the Moon, and your Breath
- Releasing Breath
- Meeting Challenges with Victory Breath
- Breath of Fire
- Alternate Nostril Breathing

"Three things cannot be long hidden: the sun, the moon, and the truth."
– Buddha

CONNECTING THE SUN, THE MOON & YOUR *Breath*

Lunar BREATH

The left nostril is connected to the Moon and your Ida Nadi. Your lunar (ida) nadi (channel) is in your subtle energy body. It controls all mental processes and the more feminine aspects of your personality. It is cooling and cleansing.

- Use if you are feeling anxious, angry, frustrated, or something similar. Perfect under the moon! Not recommended for people with low blood pressure.

Solar BREATH

The right nostril is connected to the Sun and your Pingala Nadi. Your solar (pingala) nadi (channel) is in your subtle energy body. It increases vitality and controls the more masculine aspects of your personality. It is warming and nurturing.

- Use if you are feeling tired, unmotivated, sluggish, or something similar. Perfect for sunrise and sunset too! Best done on an empty stomach. Not recommended for people with high blood pressure.

- Sit tall.
- Close your right (for Lunar) or left (for Solar) nostril with the first two fingers of your right or left hand.
- Inhale slowly and deeply through your open nostril.
- Exhale slowly through your open nostril. This is one cycle.
- Repeat 8 to 10 times or for 1 to 3 minutes.
- Allow your eyes to close while you breathe. Maybe imagine the sun or moon above your head.
- Pause after and take some deep breaths through both nostrils.
- Notice how you feel.

"When you release stress, you come home to yourself."
— Donna Eden

Releasing Breath

Releasing breath is so powerful! It helps you clear your mind, feel more in control of your emotions, and releases negative energy. It is a great way to release built-up stress.

Perfect in the afternoon when you are shifting from day to night and work to family time. It is excellent at the end of the day and really any time you feel like you need to let go of stress.

- Sit tall, either on the floor or in a chair.

- Eyes are closed. Rolled in and up towards the Third-Eye is optional.

- Cup the left hand in the right hand and let them rest in your lap.

- Begin to inhale in 4 equal sniffs. Allowing the belly to expand.

- Then take a long exhale out of your nose, drawing your navel point towards your spine.

- Repeat for 4 cycles or 1 to 3 minutes.

* Optional: If you have space, you can also take your arms out to the sides with palms up and lift them a little with each sniff. Have them touch above your head on the 4th sniff. Then you can turn your palms out and lower your arms down on the exhale.

When you finish, stomp your feet and shake your hands out.

Enjoy your calmer state of awareness!

I enjoy doing this before picking my boys up from school. It helps me release stress from my day and be more present for them.

"Whenever you need help, breathe in and mentally utter the word 'victory.' See what happens."
– Yogi Bhajan

Victory Breath

This breath is meant to be used when facing challenges. Yogi Bhajan said, "Breathe in, mentally utter the word 'Victory' and exhale. You'll find the strength of a hundred angels behind you."

It can be used as a way to stop the constant barrage of thoughts that we experience sometimes. It can also be useful when trying to lessen obsessive or addictive behavior.

This breath can be done at any time. It is unique because it does not require that you are sitting still. You can do this breathing technique while driving a car, during a conversation, when taking a test, while in a meeting, and so on. So cool!

It will help shift your focus and your mood. It is a great way to start the day, prep for meetings, deal with family, etc. This breath has helped me over and over again. It helps me stop thinking negative thoughts, change my attitude about obstacles that seem insurmountable, and helps me be open to possibilities I was resisting before.

Variation 1:
Breath in, and silently repeat the word "Victory" and then exhale.

Simple as that.

Repeat as needed or when you need a confidence boost while facing a challenge. Your eyes can be open or closed, depending on the situation.

Variation 2:
Sitting tall, inhale deeply, press the tip of your tongue to the roof of your mouth and silently repeat the word "Victory." Possibly around 3 to 4 seconds. Then exhale and let your tongue relax.

You can do this for a few rounds or set a timer for 1 to 3 minutes. You can also imagine that the word "Victory" is coming out of your third-eye chakra (brow center) as you repeat it. Imagine it either going out into the world or filling up your energy field.

Or simply finish when you feel like you have filled up your energetic space (aura) with this word and its energy or you notice a positive shift in your energy.

"With realization of one's own potential and self-confidence in one's ability, one can build a better world."
— Dalai Lama

BREATH OF Fire

When you feel like you have some major blocks to bust through, this breath will do the trick. This powerful breathing technique is known as Breath of Fire.

Once I started this practice regularly, I began to feel invincible. I truly felt like I got rid of negative energy and started vibrating at a higher level.

This breath works with your energy field and also strengthens your Solar Plexus/Navel Chakra which helps with confidence. It also clears all blocks in the chakras. This breath helps strengthen your nervous system to respond to stress with greater ease, increases lung capacity, energy, and endurance.

Use when you are feeling stuck or emotionally blocked. Also, good in the morning or for an afternoon pick-me-up.

- Sit tall with your palms up on your knees or thighs. Close your eyes.

- Inhale and expand your belly. Exhale and pull in your belly.

- Begin to do this at a quick pace. Quick sniffs and exhales of air will move through your nostrils each time. You will feel this more above your navel than below it.

- If you are not sure if you are doing it right, try sticking out your tongue and panting like a dog. After a few rounds, continue breathing like that but with your mouth closed.

- Repeat for 1 to 3 minutes. Might be less when you first start.

- To finish, take a deep inhale and hold for a moment or a count of 11 then exhale.

- Then sit for another minute or more, whatever feels best at that moment.

- Enjoy the new higher vibration you are experiencing. A tingling sensation is normal.

*Please note that it is not recommended to do this breath during pregnancy or menstruation. Also, avoid if you are prone to vertigo or have high blood pressure.

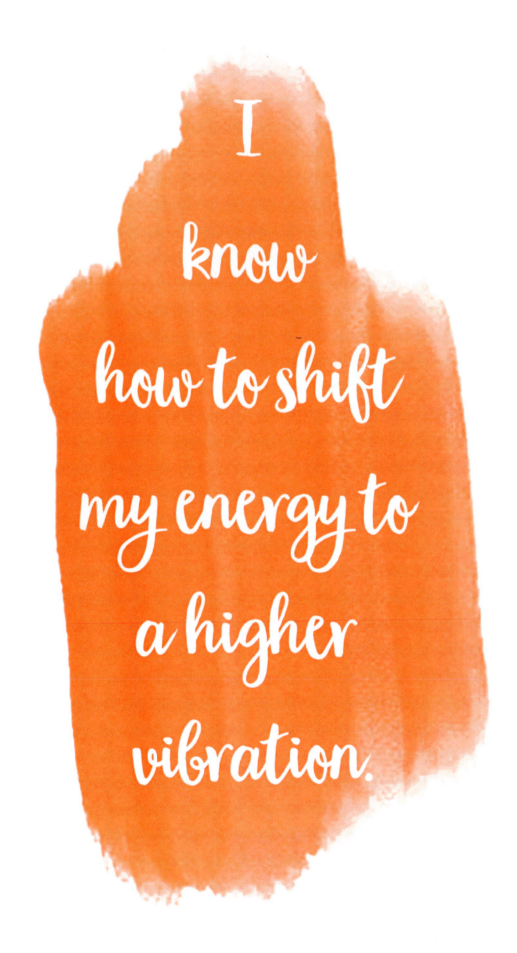

I know how to shift my energy to a higher vibration.

"Breath is King of the Mind."
— B.K.S. Iyengar

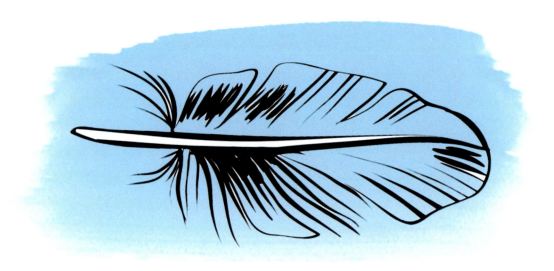

Alternate Nostril Breathing

In Sanskrit, Alternate Nostril Breathing is called Nadi Shodhana Pranayama. Remember that nadis are the channels in your subtle energy body, and pranayama is the regulation of the breath through specific techniques and exercises.

Shodhana means purification. So this breath helps clear and purify your nerves.

This is a balancing breath that is great for when you are feeling stressed or anxious.

Because this breath involves hand movement and a tremendous amount of focus, be gentle with yourself if this feels frustrating at first.

- Sit up tall with your body relaxed.

- Place your left hand with the palm facing up on your left knee.

- With your right hand, fold your middle and index fingers into your palm, allowing your thumb and your last two fingers (ring and pinky) to naturally extend out of the palm. You will alternate using your thumb to block the right nostril, and the ring and pinky fingers to block the left nostril.

- Block the left nostril, and full exhale out of the right nostril, then fully inhale. While holding the breath, close the right nostril and open the left.

- Now fully exhale out of the left nostril, and then fully inhale. While holding the breath, close the left nostril and open the right. When you exhale out of the right again, that is considered one full cycle.

- Repeat to complete 8 to 10 rounds. Or set a timer for 1 to 3 minutes.

- After the last exhale out of the right nostril, inhale deeply through both nostrils and continue with a few more deep breaths through both nostrils.

- Relax. You might want to lie down to enjoy the benefits. Enjoy how you feel.

I use my breath to create inner peace.

PART 3:
WORKING WITH YOUR *Thoughts*

SELF-LIFE COACHING EXERCISES TO HELP YOU REMOVE BLOCKS
AND SWITCH TO A MORE POSITIVE MINDSET
BY DISCOVERING WHAT MAKES YOU HAPPY,
LEARNING TO LOVE YOURSELF AS YOU ARE RIGHT NOW,
AND BELIEVING THAT YOU ARE WORTHY OF YOUR DREAMS.

"The most common way people give up their power is by thinking they don't have any."
— Alice Walker

WORKING WITH YOUR *Thoughts*

In Part 3, you will be working with your thoughts, past behaviors, negative habits and attitudes, younger self, and, most importantly, your dreams.

By the end of this section, you will appreciate how awesome you actually are, have discovered and listened to your intuition, uncovered the hopes and dreams of your younger self and your current self, released limiting beliefs you hold about yourself, revealed how your soul sees you and started to bring more of what you want into your life.

If you have ever felt stuck, lost, or wondered if this is all there is, then you are in the right place, and you are not alone. You are about to take a break from looking outside of yourself and purposefully look within yourself. This will create a positive shift in your life. Possibly, the one you have been looking for.

This section goes deeper than the other ones. You will want to use what you have learned so far to help you during these exercises. Perhaps hold a crystal during the meditation or do a breathing exercise at the beginning of a lesson. Be patient with yourself and allow yourself to answer everything honestly - this will lead to a more powerful shift.

Lessons:
- Check In
- Have Fun & Draw In
- More or Less
- Letter to Younger Self
- Thoughts Become Things
- I AM Meditation
- Dream Big

Check In

You can write your responses to the lessons in this part in a journal or use the free printable sheets found at www.kerryburki.com/free-spirit-bonuses.

You will be tempted to answer these in your head. I want you to know that the act of writing your responses down will create a greater shift and increased opportunities for healing. Especially when it comes to old wounds, it is okay to be vulnerable.

Remember that you don't have to change completely to be happy. Some things about you are personality traits and hereditary traits that are unique and beautiful.

The more self-awareness you develop, the easier it will be to learn to love yourself as you right now while working on the areas you genuinely want to change.

Use this section to tune into yourself right now.

DESCRIBE YOUR STAGE IN LIFE

Write what comes to mind - age, location, spiritual path, etc.

WHERE ARE YOU FEELING STUCK OR BLOCKED?

Think of areas in your life that you complain about and that you want to change but haven't yet.

WHERE ARE YOU FEELING JOY OR EASE?

Think of areas in your life that just run smoothly or that you are truly enjoying.

DO YOU KNOW WHAT MAKES YOU HAPPY? IF YES, WHAT?

Try not to be vague here. Put down on paper the things that make you happy. Notice if they involve making someone else happy. Be sure to write down things that bring you joy.

"When visualizing, always focus on the end result of whatever it is you want. Don't let other images enter your mind about the hows, whys, and wheres of this attainment."
– Mike Dooley

Have Fun & Draw In

This is a playful exercise that can help you shift your energy to be more open and receptive.

PICK A PLACE YOU WANT TO VISIT OR LIVE.
   Examples: Paris, Morocco, Waikiki

PICK A MOVIE YOU WOULD LIKE YOUR LIFE TO BE MORE LIKE.
   Examples: Annie Hall, Pride and Prejudice, Breakfast At Tiffany's

PICK A STYLE YOU WANT TO EMBRACE.
   Examples: Bohemian, Farmhouse, Minimalist

WHAT ARE SOME OF THE FEELINGS YOU ASSOCIATE WITH YOUR CHOICES?
   Examples: Whimsical, Calm, Retro

WHERE IN YOUR LIFE ARE YOU ALREADY EXPERIENCING THIS?
   Examples: Collection Of Berets, Macrame Wall Hangings, etc.

HOW CAN YOU BRING THE ESSENCE OF THESE INTO YOUR LIFE?
   Examples: Sleeping Mask, Mason Jars, Vintage Posters

GO BACK AND ADD TO EACH SECTION.

START TO VISUALIZE THESE EACH DAY.

THEN NOTICE IDEAS, INSPIRATION, AND OPPORTUNITIES RELATED TO THEM THAT BEGIN TO POP UP IN YOUR DAILY LIFE.

DO THIS, AGAIN AND AGAIN, TO CREATE A LIFE YOU LOVE!

I visualize my desires and draw them into my life.

"The first step to getting what you want is to have the courage to get rid of what you don't."
—Zig Ziglar

More or Less

LIST 10 THINGS YOU WANT MORE OF IN YOUR LIFE.
These can be physical things, actions, feelings, etc. Examples: quiet, goals, travel, family time, listening to intuition, money, freedom.

THEN LIST 10 THINGS YOU WANT LESS OF IN YOUR LIFE.
These can be physical things, actions, feelings, etc. Examples: low self-esteem, too many commitments, flaky friends.

PICK ONE THING FROM THE "LESS" SIDE THAT YOU WANT TO WORK ON FIRST AND CIRCLE IT.

LOOK AT YOUR "MORE" LIST AND CIRCLE WHICH 3 THINGS YOU COULD DO MORE OF TO HELP YOU HAVE LESS OF THE THING YOU CHOSE FROM THE "LESS" SIDE.
Example: When I first did this exercise, I chose to have less lack of trust in myself. I knew that more quiet, family time, and listening to my intuition would help.

TAKE THE 3 YOU ARE CHOOSING FROM THE "MORE" SIDE AND MAKE THEM ACTIONABLE STEPS YOU CAN BRING INTO YOUR LIFE GOING FORWARD.
Example: quiet = meditation, family time = scheduled/planned family activities each week, and listening to my intuition = asking my heart and God/Universe/Spirit to lead me multiple times a day.

AT THE BOTTOM OR ON ANOTHER PIECE OF PAPER, WRITE THE 3 ACTIONS.

YOU MIGHT WANT TO HANG THIS UP OR CUT OUT AND HANG THE BOTTOM PART AS A REMINDER TO DO THOSE THINGS REGULARLY. YOU COULD ALSO CREATE REMINDERS ON YOUR PHONE OR ADD THEM TO YOUR CALENDAR.

COME BACK AND DO THIS AGAIN FOR ANY OTHER ITEM ON THE "LESS" SIDE.

What I focus on expands.

"The most powerful relationship you will ever have is the one you have with yourself."
— Diane von Furstenberg

Letter To Your Younger Self

FIND AN OLD PHOTO OF YOURSELF.
Preferably one that stirs up some emotion but not one that keeps you from doing this exercise.

TAKE SOME TIME LOOKING AT THIS PHOTO.
Start to notice what feelings come up.

WRITE A LETTER TO THE YOUNGER VERSION OF YOURSELF IN THIS PHOTO.
What do you want to say to your younger self? Be honest. Get real. Don't be ashamed. This is the type of work that will help you move forward. Read this out loud to the photo of your younger self.

ALLOW ANY EMOTIONS TO COME UP. THERE IS NO WRONG WAY TO WRITE THIS LETTER.
Cry if you need to. Sometimes we have shoved our emotions down so deep, and they are still negatively affecting our lives. Allowing yourself to feel them will also allow you to release them. This can be quite healing. It can also be quite revealing.

NOW WRITE DOWN THE HOPES AND DREAMS OF YOUR YOUNGER SELF.
What do you think your younger self would want to say to your current self? What do you think your younger self wishes or hopes you have done by now or are working towards? Have these happened, or are you working on them? Can you still make them happen or have things changed?

ALLOW YOURSELF TO RELEASE GUILT AND SHAME AROUND ANYTHING YOU DIDN'T DO THAT YOU WISHED YOU HAD WHEN YOU WERE YOUNGER. FORGIVE YOURSELF.

PAT YOURSELF ON THE BACK (GO AHEAD AND DO IT!) FOR ALL OF THE THINGS YOU HAVE DONE THAT WOULD MAKE YOUR YOUNGER SELF PROUD.
Recognize any dreams you can continue with or start working on now.
Identify one thing you can do this week to make your younger self proud and do it.

"Once you replace negative thoughts with positive ones, you'll start having positive results."
— Willie Nelson

Thoughts Become Things

YOU ARE GOING TO LIST THE NEGATIVE THINGS YOU SAY TO YOURSELF REGULARLY.

Example: These can be ones you say daily - There is never enough time. I wish I were more organized. I hate my thighs. They can also be ones you say in regards to your dreams or your goals - I don't have enough money. It's hard. What if I fail?

NEXT, YOU ARE GOING TO REFRAME THESE NEGATIVE THOUGHTS INTO POSITIVE ONES.

Examples: "There is never enough time." becomes "I will find time for activities I love." "What if I fail?" becomes "What if I succeed?"

THEN, YOU WILL READ YOUR POSITIVE THOUGHTS OUT LOUD WITH EMOTION.

Notice how good it feels to say them. Embrace those feelings. Your thoughts create feelings that are felt as emotions in your heart. Those emotions create a vibrational frequency that the universe matches. Tap into positive feelings as much as possible.

HANG UP YOUR LIST OF POSITIVE THOUGHTS SO YOU REMEMBER TO SAY THEM OR KEEP THEM SOMEWHERE THAT YOU CAN READ THEM EVERY DAY. WHEN YOUR THOUGHTS AND FEELINGS GO NEGATIVE, USE THIS EXERCISE TO CREATE MORE POSITIVE EMOTIONS.

YOU CAN ALSO TAKE YOUR FAVORITE ONES AND PUT THEM IN AS REMINDERS ON YOUR PHONE, SO YOU GET DAILY ALERTS TO READ THEM.

IF YOU NEED A BIT OF EXTRA HELP, PICK ONE OF THESE RELEASING AFFIRMATIONS TO REPEAT DAILY.

I release old habits and choose new positive ones.
Obstacles are now falling away quickly.
I lovingly release my negative thoughts and choose positive ones.
I willingly release old beliefs and actively create new supportive ones.
I release thoughts that no longer serve me.
I transform negative energy into love and light.

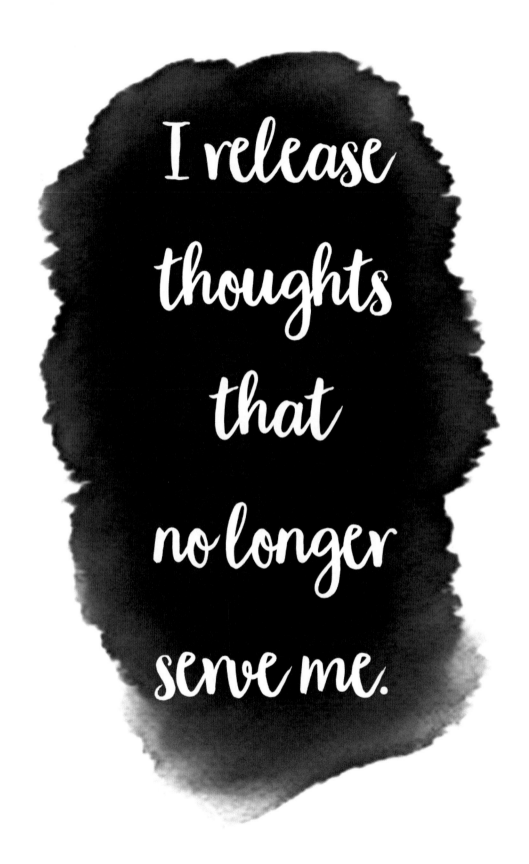

"Be nice to yourself. It's hard to be happy, when someone is being mean to you all of the time."
— Christine Arylo

I AM meditation

Let's allow your inner knowing (your soul, your spirit, your intuition, your higher self) to voice the truth about your authentic self. Set aside some quiet time to do this. Possibly play some music in the background, light some candles, burn some incense. You can sit tall and close your eyes or lie down. Get comfortable.

BEGIN TO REPEAT "I AM (YOUR NAME)."

Do this out loud or silently at least 10 times. This can be your first and last name or just your first name or your full name. Notice what thoughts come up.

THEN BEGIN TO REPEAT "I AM _____."

Allow yourself to fill in the blank with words that describe you. Focus on the positive. Release any negative words that come up. Examples: Loving, Wise, Beautiful. Write down the positive ones.

NOW, BEGIN TO REPEAT "SHE WHO" OR "HE WHO" OR "THEY WHO."

Notice what words come up. Write them down. Again, focus on the positive. Release any negative words that come up. Examples: follows her heart, gives freely, embraces life.

ARE YOUR CURRENT ACTIONS ALIGNED WITH WHAT CAME UP?

IS THERE ANYTHING YOU CAN DO IN THE NEAR FUTURE TO ALIGN YOUR LIFE WITH THESE TRUTHS?

WRITE THEM DOWN AND ACT ON THEM.

I am loving, wise, and beautiful.

"The future belongs to those who believe in the beauty of their dreams."
— Eleanor Roosevelt

Dream Big

WHAT IS YOUR BIG DREAM?
Write it out in full detail. Can you add to it? Jot down a few more details.

CAN YOU GO BIGGER?
You know you can. Write down some things that take it to the next level. Go for it!

CHECK IN WITH YOURSELF TO SEE IF YOU ARE HOLDING BACK.
If you think you are coming too much from your head, take a moment to breathe or move your body a bit. This will help you get into your heart. Maybe even close your eyes, and take some deep breaths with your hand on your heart.

NOW GO BIG! DON'T HOLD BACK. REMEMBER, THERE ARE NO LIMITS TO YOUR BIG DREAM.

NOW READ WHAT YOU WROTE AND GET EXCITED!

REWRITE THE WHOLE THING AS THOUGH IT IS HAPPENING RIGHT NOW.
THEN RECORD YOURSELF READING THIS VERSION OUT LOUD USING YOUR PHONE.
Example: "I dream of doing volunteer work in the rainforest." becomes "I am living my dream and doing volunteer work in the rainforest." Then find a place to get comfortable and play it back while you listen with your eyes closed. Begin to imagine everything you wrote with great detail. Imagine the colors, smells, and feelings. Notice how this makes you feel. Notice if any ideas pop into your head that you can take action on to make your big dreams come true.

VISUALIZE YOUR BIG DREAM ONCE A DAY FOR A FEW MINUTES, IMAGINING ALL OF THE DETAILS. WRITE DOWN OR ASK OUT LOUD: "WHAT IS THE NEXT RIGHT STEP TOWARDS MAKING MY DREAMS COME TRUE?" HAVE A NOTEBOOK NEARBY TO WRITE DOWN ANY IDEAS OR INSPIRATIONS THAT POP UP.

YOU MIGHT LIKE TO READ WHAT YOU WROTE BEFORE YOU VISUALIZE TOO. YOU CAN ALSO LISTEN TO THE RECORDING AS YOUR MORNING PRACTICE OR ANY TIME YOU ARE FEELING FEARFUL, STUCK, OR UNMOTIVATED.

Kerry Burki - Free Spirit Guidebook

I am not too old to set a new goal or dream a new dream.

Part 4:
WORKING WITH YOUR
Imagination & Energy

GO FROM COPING TO THRIVING BY USING TECHNIQUES TO HELP YOU WORRY LESS, TRUST YOURSELF MORE, AND FEEL CONNECTED TO YOURSELF & THE UNIVERSE.

"Logic will get you from A to B. Imagination will take you everywhere."
— Albert Einstein

Working with your Imagination & Energy

In Part 4, you will be working with energy and unseen forces. These lessons will strengthen your connection to yourself and the universe.

This section requires you to have an open mind. The results will not always be immediate or tangible. If you can relax and be open to a new way of living, these lessons can get you and keep you in the flow of life. They can help you live with more grace, more joy, and more ease.

By the end of this section, you will know how to feel grounded, have a connection to guides and angels in your life, be working with your energy centers and your energy field, have a stronger connection to your intuition and your true self.

These techniques might take you out of your comfort zone, and I want you to know that that is where the magic lies.

"Nothing in life is to be feared, it is only to be understood. Now is the time to understand more, so that we may fear less." - Marie Curie

Lessons:
- Get Grounded
- Tap into your Intuition
- Working with Animal Guides
- Working with your Runners
- Color Energy
- Naming Your Higher Self
- Working with Angels
- Clearing Visualization
- Protection Visualization
- Knowing your Chakras
- Living by the Light of the Moon

"Get yourself grounded and you can navigate even the stormiest roads in peace."
– Steve Goodier

GET Grounded

I am so excited to share this grounding technique that I learned over 20 years ago while I was in college.

This exercise is the perfect way to start your day. Also, you can do this on the fly on those days when you feel super busy. It is a great technique to ground you in the present moment when life feels overwhelming, or your head is in the clouds.

Find a comfortable place to sit to do this exercise. On the days you forget, you can do it on the go.

Imagine a cord or rope or root connected to the base of your spine. As you take deep breaths, imagine this cord/rope/root getting longer and longer. Imagine it going through the floor below you, then the grass, and dirt. Imagine it going deep into the center of the earth. With each breath, imagine it going deeper until it reaches the earth's core.

Imagine it encompassing and becoming one with the center of the earth. You can imagine the core as a large rock or crystal. Feel a gentle yet firm pull on the base of your spine.

Know that you are connected to the earth's energy right now.

Imagine anything that you feel like you need from the earth like energy, stability, comfort, resources, or mothering is drawing up the cord/rope/root and flowing through you.

If you imagine a root, you can also imagine offshoots of the root spreading through the earth to help you feel even more connected and rooted.

Notice how grounded you feel.

Anytime you lose this feeling, imagine that cord/rope/root connecting you to the energy of the earth and breathe.

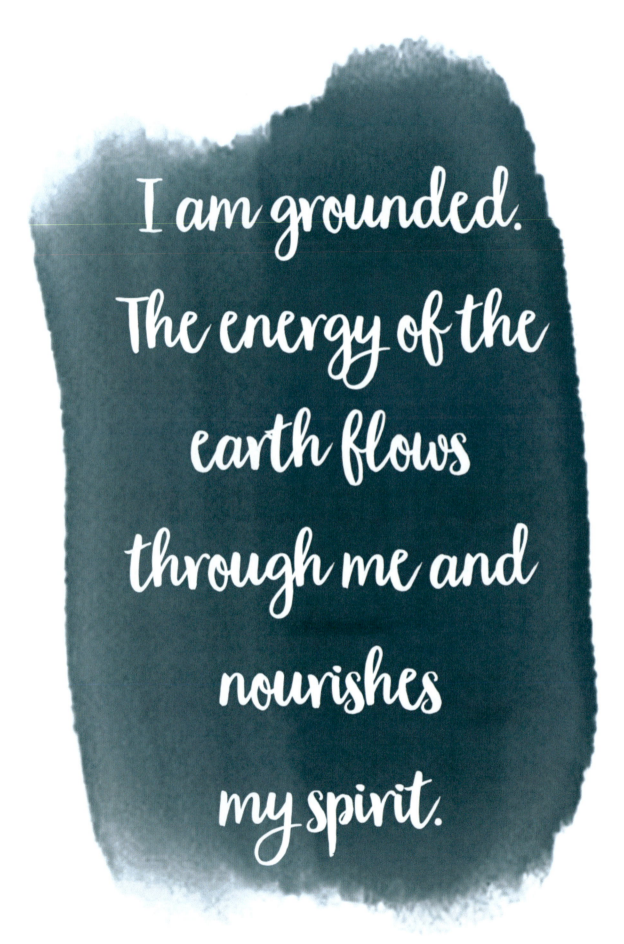

I am grounded. The energy of the earth flows through me and nourishes my spirit.

"Don't try to comprehend with your mind.

Your minds are very limited.

Use your intuition."

– Madeleine L'Engle

TAPPING INTO YOUR *Intuition*

The definition of intuition is a thing that one knows or considers likely from instinctive feeling rather than conscious reasoning. This meditation will get you into a state of trusting your intuitive feelings and also find a place where you can tap into them with ease.

On the next page, there are a few activities you can do after the meditation. Please wait until after you have gone through the meditation once before reading about them.

Sit tall or lie down. Read through the meditation and then let your mind take you through it or listen to my recording by visiting www.kerryburki.com/free-spirit-bonuses.

Imagine you are standing at the top of a spiral staircase. Feel the railing in your hand. Notice if it is cool or warm to the touch. Slowly spiral down the stairs. Feel each step beneath your feet. After spiraling multiple times, you come to the bottom and step into a beautiful natural setting. One that makes you feel whole. Maybe you have been here before, maybe you dream of going here, or maybe you have never seen this place before.

Begin to follow the path in front of you. Look around and notice your surroundings. Take in the sights and smells. Maybe touch a tree or smell a flower. Enjoy this walk.

Take the path until you find the perfect place to sit or lie down. Notice that you feel calm. Know that you are exactly where you are supposed to be.

Relax in this space that you have chosen to get in touch with your intuition. Become aware of the fact that all of the answers you seek are here if you want them. Put out into the universe a question you have or an area of your life you desire guidance around. Notice if any words or impressions come right away.

If nothing comes, know that the answers and opportunities will show up at the right time and that you will remain open to receiving them.

After a while, get up and go back to the path. Walk along until you get to the bottom of the staircase. Begin to climb and spiral up, up, up. Feel the steps under your feet and the railing in your hand.

When you get to the top, take a deep breath. Feel gratitude for your life, your body, your mind, and your connection to the universe.

This might end up being your go-to meditation when you are feeling like you are spending too much time looking outside of yourself for answers or haven't been trusting yourself much lately.

I recommend that you do this meditation at least once. If you enjoy it, then please do it more than once. I would suggest weekly after that or when you feel called to do it.

PLEASE READ AFTER YOU DO THE MEDITATION:

- Take some time to write down the details of your meditation.

- Notice if the place was somewhere you have been, somewhere known, or somewhere new to you.

- In the future, notice if you go back to the same place or if you visit new ones.

- Take note of feelings in the body. Example: When I do this meditation, I feel it in my stomach. Note: I almost feel myself going down the stairs there. It is wild. It helped me learn that my intuition has a strong connection to my Solar Plexus Chakra. Now I know to trust the feelings that I experience there in my daily life.

- When you are feeling overwhelmed and don't have time to do this meditation, remember that you can still visualize yourself at the same place you visit in the meditation. It is within you always.

Go there often.

This meditation can open up new worlds to you.

Allow it.

Allow all of the lessons in this guide to help you deepen your intuition.

Getting quiet and paying attention are two important aspects that will help you make the switch to living more intuitively.

>>> *The benefits are less worry and more trust in yourself.* <<<

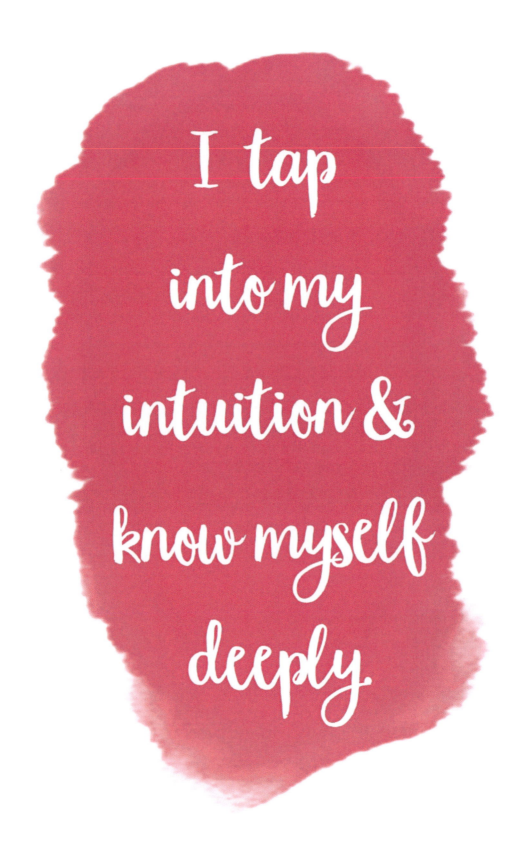

"Some people talk to animals. Not many listen though. That's the problem."
— A.A. Milne

WORKING WITH
Animal Guides

Working with animal guides can change your life!

Every animal has different energies associated with them that we can connect with and get energy from at different points in our life.

Many years ago, during a shamanic healing session with a friend, a bear showed up in my meditation. A month later, the bear showed up again during a meditation at home. I took it as a sign and started working with this bear. This was a surprise to me because I had always associated myself with tigers.

Once I researched some of the meanings and energies associated with bears, I knew that that was what I truly needed at that time in my life. I am sharing this as a reminder to stay open to what shows up. I believe it is possible to work with many different animals throughout your life.

I have created a meditation that will open you up to connecting with the animal and energy you need right now.

You will feel supported and connected.

Depending on your current situation, you might like to do this meditation regularly to work with new animals, or you might want to stick with one animal for a while.

Listen to your intuition.

I suggest reading through the meditation and then either lie down or sit comfortably.

You can let your mind take you through it or listen to my recording by visiting www.kerryburki.com/free-spirit-bonuses.

Animal Guide Meditation

Imagine that you are walking on a path in a beautiful natural setting.

What is the path made of? Dirt, sand, gravel? What is on your feet? Shoes, boots, nothing? Feel the earth beneath you with each step.

Take some time to look around and notice the details that are around you.

What do you see? Bushes, trees, flowers? What do you hear? Wind, birds, water? What do you feel? A breeze, humidity, the ground under your feet? What do you smell? Saltwater, jasmine, pine trees?

Enjoy your surroundings and know that you are exactly where you are supposed to be.

Notice a clearing up ahead. Once you are there, find a place to get comfortable. Allow your mind to think about the stage of life that you are in right now.

Ask for guidance. "I would love some guidance in my life right now." or "I am open to receiving guidance about _____." Fill in the blank with a more specific situation like looking for a new job, raising my children, or mending a relationship.

Then trust that the guidance will come. Take a look around and see if an animal has shown up. If one has, begin to make a connection.

There is a sense of safety here. You either move towards the animal or maybe it comes to you. Depending on the animal, you can pet it, look into its eyes, or simply feel its energy.

If no animal shows up, then keep an eye out in your daily life for an animal that seems to be showing up regularly in images, messages, or in real life.

Know that this animal is your guide. It will be at your side to support you.

You can now go back to the path, knowing that you are now or soon will be working with your animal guide.

Again, notice your surroundings, walk tall, smile, and know that you are supported.

You can come back to this natural setting any time you want for relaxation, to get away, or to connect deeper with your animal guide.

The next few pages share some of the common animal guides that show up for people and their corresponding energies. I also recommend doing an internet search or finding books or oracle cards about animal guides to take this work deeper.

If no animal showed up in your meditation, here are a few ways to discover your animal guide:

1. Start paying attention to animals that you notice repeatedly. This could be during meditations, in magazines, on tv, in real life, etc.

2. Read through the descriptions of the energies associated with the animals on the following pages. Note if one jumps out at you that you could really benefit from in your life right now.

3. Separate the animal cards from the printable oracle card deck that is part of the bonuses of this guidebook (www.kerryburki.com/free-spirit-bonuses). Hold them in front of your heart and ask which animal you need in your life right now. Either shuffle the cards until you intuitively feel like stopping and pick the top one, or shuffle until one falls out, or lay all the cards face down and with your right hand on your heart and your left hand moving over the cards and pick the one intuitively feel drawn to.

When you are ready to connect and work with your animal, imagine that you are standing next to the animal you need. Put your hand on the animal.

Know that you are safe. Imagine the energy you want to tap into coming from the animal and merging with you.

Take a moment to thank the animal and know that you can connect to their energy at any time.

Going forward you can choose to interact with your animal guide on a regular basis. You can ask for guidance, ask it to take your worries away, ask it to give you a sign, and so much more. Let your imagination run wild and create your own ways of working with your animal guide.

Have fun with this!

My bear wears a flower crown, and I LOVE it!

You can also name your animal if you feel called to or if a name pops up for you.

Animal Guides

Bear
Hibernation. Solitude. Alone time. Protection. Mama bear. Grounded. Earth energy. Strength. Confidence.

Fox
Trickster. Swiftly maneuvers around obstacles. Quick thinking. Physical prowess. Great at facing sticky situations.

Hummingbird
Looking for & enjoying the sweetness of life. Lightness of being. Adaptability. Independence & swiftness. Air energy.

Squirrel
Perseverance. Active Life. Hardworking. Planning ahead. Resourceful.

Dog
Luck. Love. Protection. Loyalty. Unconditional Love. Playfulness. Reliability.

Bull
Two types of energy: Grounded and Content & Strong and Charged up. Which energy showed up or which one do you need?

Monkey
Resourcefulness. Curiosity and Energy. Allow more playfulness into your life.

Unicorn
Luck. Magic. Fantasy. Manifesting. Beauty. Dreams. Angel connection. Purity.

Animal Guides

Lion
Powerful. Strength. Personal power. Assertiveness. Dominate. Regal. King-like. Fire energy.

Wolf
Protection. Guardian. Be fierce. Lead your pack. Trust your instincts. Social connections. Howl.

Snake
Life force energy (Kundalini). Transformation. Earth energy. Starting fresh. Shedding old ways.

Llama
Go slow and work hard. Persevere when feeling burdened or overwhelmed. Curious and Unique.

Sea Turtle
Good luck. Longevity. Peace. Emotional strength. Water Energy. Navigating currents of life with ease.

Don't worry about what others think. Trust your instincts. Earth energy. Good luck. Happiness. Beware of greedy tendencies.

Giraffe
Seeing life from a unique point of view. Self-love. Proud of appearance. May have to stick neck out to get what you want.

Crow
Mysticism and Magic. Sign of change. Learn how to be true to yourself. Clever. Trickster.

Kerry Burki - Free Spirit Guidebook

Animal Guides

Butterfly

Transformation. Whimsy. Renewal and rebirth. Lightness of being. Bright colors.

Turtle

Slow and steady. Protected. Pace yourself. Long life. Take a break. Longevity. Home is wherever you are.

Bee

Self-mastery comes from hard, diligent work. Good luck. Creating sweetness in life. Abundance.

Deer

Invitation for gentleness and compassion. Possibly towards yourself or another. Regeneration. Sensitivity.

Horse

Personal drive. Is it wild or tamed? Yin and yang parts of you? Inner strength. Passionate.

Owl

Wisdom. Intuition. Sacred Knowledge. Ability to navigate in the dark (metaphor). See what is hidden to most.

Spider

Mystery. Feminine energy. Creativity. Are you caught in a web or weaving your own destiny? Patience. Shadow self.

Hawk

Time to look at the whole picture. Learn to be more discerning. Focus. Power. Vision. Air energy.

Kerry Burki - Free Spirit Guidebook

Animal Guides

Elephant

Gentle power. Discover your role in your pack. Strength. Family. Royalty.

Dolphin

Intelligence. Instincts. Water energy. Going with the flow. Peace. Playfulness. Gentleness.

Cat

Luck. Mix of independence and affection. Waiting for the right moment to act. Deep sense of self. Curiosity.

Frog

Cleansing. Water energy. Transformations and Transitions. Create and follow steps towards goals.

Buffalo

You have everything you need. Abundance. Stability. Prayer and Gratitude.

Rabbit

Fertility. Creativity. Luck. Abundance. Cleverness. Pay attention to the world around you.

Eagle

Efforts aligned with the divine. Soar to unimaginable heights. See the larger picture. Strength and freedom. Sexual energy and mate for life.

Camel

Journey. Ready for the long haul. Travel. Self-Sufficient. Stamina. Possibly time to find and rest at an oasis.

I am open to the energy, messages, and wisdom of my animal guides.

"As you think you vibrate. As you vibrate you attract."
— Abraham Hicks

WORKING WITH YOUR *Runners*

Runners are guides that will help you locate lost items, get parking spots, bring things into your life that you desire, and more.

It is fairly simple. Say you have lost your keys and you are searching frantically. Pause and ask your Runners to find the keys for you. Notice any thoughts that pop into your head after.

The main thing you are doing here is shifting your energy. You are going from a state of resisting what you want to a state of being open and expecting it come to you.

When you can match the energy that you desire, the things you desire can start to flow into your life with ease.

Working with Runners is a good way to get into a habit of shifting your energy so you can begin manifesting larger life goals down the line.

Ask your Runners to get something for you this week.

Decide what you would like to call your Runner guides if you prefer something different. Feel free to choose something that makes you happy.

To keep the positivity flowing, you might consider carrying a small notebook so you can track results, celebrate, and give thanks.

Have fun with this! Make it a game. I have my children do this with parking spots all of the time. Get creative as time goes by and you will begin to feel like Runners are some of your best friends to have around.

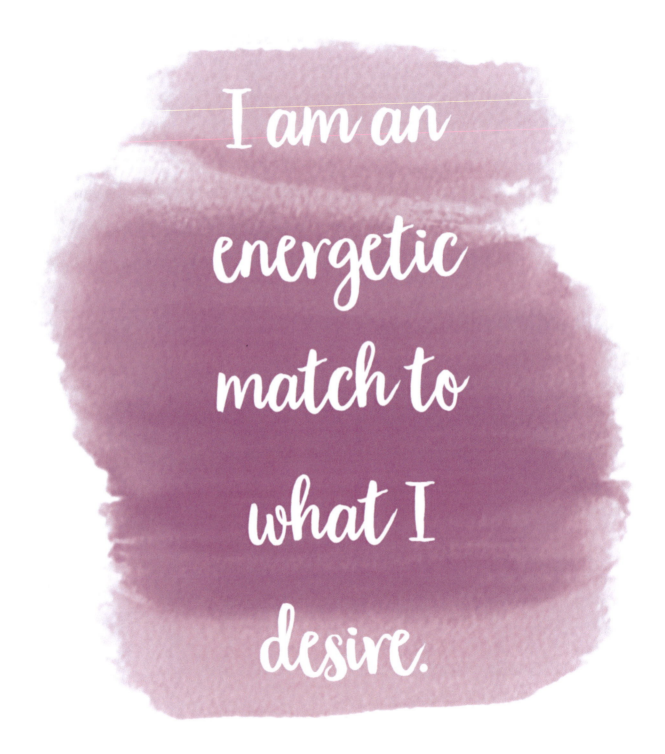

I am an energetic match to what I desire.

"Color is a power which directly influences the soul."
— Wassily Kandinsky

Color
ENERGY

You already have a strong connection to color. Think about the colors you absolutely adore. Now think about the colors that make you go "blah." I love how they can be different for everyone!

Some of these associations are simply natural like you were born with them. Others have developed over time due to life experiences.

Either way, you already have a deep understanding of the power of color. Now it is time to bring that power into your daily life.

Here are some simple ways to use color to create a life you love. The following page is a color chart that you might like to print out and hang, laminate, or put somewhere as a reminder (www.kerryburki.com/free-spirit-bonuses).

Clothing - Start dressing for your mood or the mood you want to embody that day. Notice what is missing in your wardrobe. Some of the colors missing you might be okay with and others you might want to consider bringing in to help you feel more of the qualities associated with it.

Decor - Look around your home and notice the dominant colors. Maybe add in other secondary colors to bring about a different vibe in your home. It is also nice to switch colors with the seasons. Use the guide when picking candles out too.

Aura - Look at the energy of each color and choose one that relates to how you want to feel that day. Then close your eyes and imagine a sphere of that color surrounds you and fills you with its light and energy. You have an energy field around you called your aura. It is projected out into the world and often what other people pick up on when they run into you, or when you enter a room. Being more intentional about how you want to feel and what you want to project is very empowering.

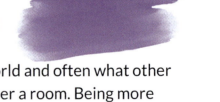

Pay attention to other ways color plays a role in your life. Enjoy!

Color Energy

PINK
Love, intuitive energy, compassion, hope, sensitivity, nurturing.

RED
Grounding, security, power, passion, luck.
Root Chakra

ORANGE
Emotions, creativity, adventure, happiness.
Sacral Chakra

YELLOW
Energy, vitality, optimism, inner strength.
Solar Plexus (Navel) Chakra

GREEN
Love, balance, growth, luck, health, nature.
Heart Chakra

BLUE
Communication, peace, loyalty, healing.
Throat Chakra

INDIGO
Intuition, understanding, integrity, truth.
Third-Eye (Brow) Chakra

VIOLET
Spirituality, wisdom, imagination, magic.
Crown Chakra

BLACK
Power, death, elegance, mystery, protection, sophistication, negativity.

BROWN
Home, comfort, outdoors, stability.
Earth energy.

GOLD
Prosperity, luxury, abundance, spirituality.
Solar Energy

SILVER
Calming, reflection, intuition, glamour.
Lunar energy

WHITE
Divinity, light, angels, cleansing, protection.
Crown Chakra and Aura

I choose colors that my soul craves and they help me heal.

"Take a moment today and purposefully connect with your higher self. It is the part of you that is always connected with source. It is filled with love, compassion and wisdom. It holds no judgment or fear. It is you in your purest form of light."
– Laurel Bleadon-Maffei

NAMING YOUR Higher Self

When you are seeking guidance or direction it can be so much more fun when you have a name for your higher self. When you think of your higher self, I want you to think of yourself on an energetic level, the version of yourself you think of when you tune into your heart and soul.

I like to picture my higher self as a bright light above my head. You might already have a different interpretation and that is wonderful.

If you don't have any sort of connection or idea of your higher self, try the activity below and then simply allow it to emerge over time and stay open to what shows up.

Close your eyes and take some time imagining yourself as light. See this light as the truest and purest version of yourself. The version of yourself that is not defined by your birth name, the color of your skin, where you live, etc.

Once you get this image of yourself as light, notice if a name shows up.

Stay open to any possibilities. You might get hints later for the name of your higher self from a song, or a billboard, or even a dream.

Now have fun! When you are stuck or feeling lost, ask your higher self for guidance. Pay attention to synchronicities that show up.

When you are feeling particularly lost or frustrated, take some deep breaths, ask what your higher self would do in this situation.

This will help you live from your heart and soul and less from your head and society's influences.

Kerry Burki - Free Spirit Guidebook - 106

"Angels are principally the guardians of our spirits. Their function is not to do our work for us, but to help us do it ourselves."
— Eileen Elias Freeman

WORKING WITH Angels

I started working with angels about 5 years ago and it has helped ease my anxiety so much. Once I started to visualize them and ask for their help, I discovered that my worries would melt away. Here are a few ways to get started:

- Ask angels to watch over someone. You can even imagine an angel over them and protecting them. Perfect for bedtime and after watching the news.
- When driving a car or traveling anywhere, ask angels to get you there safely while also keeping everyone around you safe. You can imagine the angels around the vehicle.
- Imagine a circle of angels around your house and clearing it with light. Then imagine them staying around the house and protecting it.
- Ask angels to guide you through your day. In the morning, wake up and say, "Angels, please guide me today."
- Ask angels to take your worries away. Give your worries to your angels and ask for the solutions needed to appear.
- Remember to thank angels for their help.

Play around with working with angels. Keep it light and fun if you are new to this. If you have been doing this for a while, then take this opportunity to deepen your connection by asking your angels for signs.

It might be hard for you to trust that they are helping at first but learning how to release control is part of how this works.

It's all about asking and not assuming. People assume that if there are angels, then why aren't they always helping. A lot of this has to do with energy. When we ask angels to help, that energy goes into the universe and is matched.

You have to learn how to raise your vibration and not get stuck in negativity. You are the one doing the work here.

Consider finding some angel imagery to place around to help remind you of their presence.

"It's transformative to clear your life of the heavy stuff that is weighing you down."
— Dana Claudat

Clearing
VISUALIZATION

You are more powerful than you think. You can use your mind to raise or lower your mood and vibration at any time.

Sometimes we are caught off guard and find ourselves filled with worry or angst. Most of these times are due to circumstances that have happened outside of ourselves, and then our ego takes hold, and our mind gets on a roll of saying fearful and false things.

Your body might feel bogged down or antsy. Your energy might be frenetic or cranky.

These are the times when you will want to clear your energy.

Start by trying this once at the end of your day. This is simple and quick enough for you to do right before you go to sleep. Then begin to do this whenever you feel like you are carrying other people's junk. You might simply feel out of sorts, or in a funk, or cranky.

Begin to pay attention to when you feel like you have picked up negative energy. Just becoming aware of the fact that you feel out of alignment and that you are dealing with a lot that does not serve you will have you feeling empowered and less like a victim of the world around you.

Special note: Sometimes when you are feeling junky or negative, it means that something has bubbled to the surface that needs attention. You can keep clearing it, but it will come back until you face it. Learn to trust your intuition in these situations.

Clearing
VISUALIZATION

Imagine one of the following moving down from above your head, through and around your body (front, back, sides, top, and bottom) until you feel like you and the space around you have been cleared.

1. A ball of white light (or any color).

2. The sun. Imagine heat and flames from the sun moving down and through you burning away and clearing anything that is not serving you.

3. A silvery full moon. Imagine it's cooling energy just dissolving and clearing any energy that is not yours.

4. Stars. Imagine that the energy within and around you after is sparkly and bright.

It is nice to imagine the energy being transmuted into neutral energy. You might like to finish by saying "An aura of positive energy surrounds and infuses my body."

Other options are imagining a magic wand moving around you and magically clearing your space.

Sometimes I like to picture angels blowing any junk I have picked up out of my energy field.

Breathing exercises, dancing, singing, showers, and baths with this intention can really help you feel a shift also.

Spend some time finding favorite ways to clear yourself on a regular basis. Try to make it special and nurturing so that you can reconnect with your innate positive energy.

I choose to clear the negative energy around me and connect with my positive vibrations.

"Energy is contagious, positive and negative alike. I will forever be mindful of what and who I am allowing into my space."
— Alex Elle

Protection
VISUALIZATION

Every day is filled with events, attitudes, opinions, people, news, and more that require your attention. It is easy to feel drained or overwhelmed if you feel like it is your responsibility to take it all in and deal with it.

When you intentionally protect yourself each day, you can limit what enters your energy field and interact with the world from a place of love. Visualizing a protective space around you makes it easier not to react to every little thing that happens.

It gives you the space to breathe and decide how you want to respond, which in turn helps you live with more intention and not just allowing the actions of others to dictate your life.

Begin by closing your eyes and imagining a sphere of bright white light all around you. Imagine it as a beautiful, loving barrier protecting you from negativity, fear, chaos, etc.

You can also imagine yourself in a situation in which you know you would like some protection. Imagine yourself interacting but not absorbing anything being said or being energetically sent to you. A fun way to do this is imagining the light as a bubble. Picture anything that you don't want entering your bubble bouncing off.

You might like to repeat in your mind: I am protected, or I am divinely protected.

Once your eyes open, know that the light is around you and you are still protected. You can change the color to suit your moods or needs.

Try doing this first thing in the morning, so you feel protected for the day. You might also like to do a quick version while in your car, before entering meetings, before phone calls, and so on. Play around with this and have fun.

Maybe you imagine yourself putting up your wrists like Wonder Woman deflecting negativity or spinning around with a magic wand keeping your space protected. You can even imagine a small ball of light starting at your heart and growing until it surrounds you.

"The body is the vehicle, consciousness the driver. Yoga is the path, and the chakras are the map."
— Anodea Judith

KNOWING YOUR Chakras

I started working with chakras when I began my yoga practice in 1997. My practice has evolved, and I still work with them daily.

This lesson will be more of an overview so you can begin to think about and work with the chakras in your own life. If you are familiar with your chakras, then I hope this helps you reconnect with them or deepen your connection.

Chakra means "wheel" or "circle" in Sanskrit and refers to spinning wheels of energy found in your subtle energy body (not your physical body). For most people, these centers are constricted. That means life force energy (Prana) is not flowing through them easily.

When you begin to open them up, energy can travel from them throughout your energy body in channels called nadis. This gives you access to more energy and higher states of consciousness.

The primary nadi is the Sushumna and corresponds with your spinal column. It is here that you find your 7 main chakras.

Use the chart on the following pages to learn about each chakra.

When you want to focus on a specific chakra, you can visualize its corresponding color as light in that area of your body then repeat the affirmation associated with that chakra or chant the sound associated with the chakra.

Visualize all the chakras glowing brightly in your body for an immediate energy boost!

Yoga poses are designed to help clear and balance the chakras.

Chakras

7th Chakra - Crown - Sahasrara - Violet/White - Top of Head - Thought/Consciousness - Associated with Divinity and Enlightenment - Blocked = Attachment - **Sound** = Silence - **Affirmation:** I am one with everything.

6th Chakra - Third Eye - Ajna - Indigo - Between Eyebrows - Light - Associated with Intuition and Imagination - Blocked = Illusion - **Sound** = OM (ohm) - **Affirmation:** I am intuitive and follow my inner guidance.

5th Chakra - Throat - Vishuddha - Blue - Throat - Sound - Associated with Communication and Expression - Blocked = Lies - **Sound** = HAM (hahm) - **Affirmation:** I express my truth with ease.

4th Chakra - Heart - Anahata - Green - Heart Center - Air - Associated with Love and Relationships - Blocked = Grief - **Sound** = YAM (yahm) - **Affirmation:** I am loving and lovable.

3rd Chakra: Solar Plexus - Manipura - Yellow - Above navel - Fire - Associated with Confidence and Will Power - Blocked = Shame - **Sound** = RAM (rahm) - **Affirmation:** I like myself and stand in my power.

2nd Chakra - Sacral - Svadhishthana - Orange - Below navel - Water - Associated with Sexuality and Creativity - Blocked = Guilt - **Sound** = VAM (vahm) - **Affirmation:** I express myself in loving and positive ways.

1st Chakra - Root - Muladhara - Red - Base of Spine - Earth - Associated with Security and Groundedness - Blocked = Fear - **Sound** = LAM (lahm) - **Affirmation:** I am safe and connected to the earth.

Chakras

Use this chart to help you discover if you are deficient or excessive in each chakra. You might be on both sides for some chakras, and that is okay. This is a lesson in awareness. Use the tips at the beginning of this lesson to help balance each chakra.

Deficient: Cynicism, depression rigid, apathy.

Excessive: Egomaniac, overly intellectual, spiritual obsession, confusion.

Deficient: Unclear thought, deluded, lack of imagination, insensitivity.

Excessive: Hallucinations, obsessions, nightmares, difficulty concentrating.

Deficient: Secretive, creatively stuck, shyness, fear of speaking.

Excessive: Hurtful or excessive speech, judgment, poor listening skills.

Deficient: Anti-social, lack of empathy, critical.

Excessive: Poor boundaries, jealousy, people-pleaser.

Deficient: Low self-esteem, weak will power, blames others, lack of energy.

Excessive: Egotistical, overly-ambitious, selfish, angry, competitive, stubborn.

Deficient: Codependent, submissive, martyr, lack of passion, avoidance of pleasure.

Excessive: Manipulative, overly sexual, controlling, ruled by emotions, mood swings.

Deficient: Scattered, anxiety, victim-mentality, fearful, underweight, restless.

Excessive: Greed, overweight, sluggish, overly-protective, workaholic, hoarding.

"darling, the moon is still the moon in all of its phases."
— isra al-thibeh

LIVING BY THE LIGHT OF THE *Moon*

This lesson holds a special place in my heart. When I first started following the moon, I simply began by noticing the phases. I got a thrill from looking up and knowing that a full moon was on its way or that I was seeing the last sliver before a new moon.

I started learning more and loved discovering that there was different energy associated with each phase. I was never one to set monthly or yearly goals. I was always in the moment. Sometimes though that meant I floated along without intention. Working with each phase helped me focus on goals I wanted to reach, habits or tendencies I wanted to release, and an opportunity to be grateful for it all.

When you start paying attention to what phase the moon is in and living by that phase, you will begin to feel a connection to something much larger than yourself.

You will feel connected to nature, your intuition, the universe, the moon, the sun, the divine, your desires, and to other people and animals around the planet.

This lesson will share the qualities and energy associated with each major moon phase plus some activities to help you set intentions or start new projects or simply spend time with the moon.

You will begin to get out of your head, look up to the sky, and look within for guidance and peace. Have fun with this knowledge. You might like to follow the moon every month, or you might be the type to do it every so often.

Listen to your heart and try not to let this information overwhelm you. You can make this as simple or elaborate as your heart desires. Just remember, that will change too just like the phases of the moon!

Allow the phases of the moon to remind you that you go through phases too. During each lunar cycle, during each year, and throughout your life.

Learn to honor your phases and yourself.

Moon Phases

Use this Moon Phase Guide to remind you of each phase. There is a printable version and a Manifesting with the Moon worksheet to help you set intentions and keep track of your efforts at www.kerryburki.com/free-spirit-bonuses. My favorite place to find the dates for each phase is here: www.timeanddate.com/moon/phases/.

NEW MOON

This is an ideal time for setting new intentions and beginning new projects. The moon is between the earth and the sun causing it to be hidden from view because the dark side is facing earth.

intention setting new beginnings

The New Moon is always in the current astrological sign. The energy lasts about 3 1/2 days.

Intention Setting:
Write down your intention starting with "I am" or "I intend." Some examples: "I intend to work with my animal guide." or "I will be more forgiving towards myself."

You can write this in a journal or on your bonus worksheet.

Say your intention out loud. How would you feel if these statements were true? Tap into that feeling. Visualize what it would look like. Do this daily during the moon cycle for extra energy around your intention.

You can plan out the lunar cycle by filling out the bonus worksheet during the New Moon. This will guide you during the phases.

WAXING MOON

thoughtful action todo list

This is a time for taking action. This is the phase when the moon is "growing." When you look up at the moon and the right side is what you see, it is in the waxing phase. This includes Waxing Crescent, First Quarter (Half Moon), and Waxing Gibbous.

Thoughtful actions in regards to your intention or project are great during this phase. Write down ideas and actions on a todo list or your bonus worksheet. Examples: Be on the lookout for your animal guide. Notice self-defeating thoughts. Repeat positive affirmations.

Daily: Act as if your intention is already a reality. Meaning maybe you would check in with your animal guide every morning, complain less, dress with more confidence, not put yourself down, etc.

FUll MOON

The moon is shining at its brightest. If possible, find time to be out under the moonlight. This is a time for celebration and gratitude.

Ritual: Find time on the night of the full moon or the 3 days before or after to do yoga poses, breathing exercises, say affirmations, or light candles. Express gratitude for your life and your intention or project at this time. This is powerful! You can write out your ritual on your bonus worksheet if you like.

Take note of any manifestations or guidance that have shown up so far and celebrate.

Possibly journal about thoughts, emotions, or ideas to help you get even more guidance.

If you are feeling overwhelmed, you might like to simply sit under the light of the moon.

WaNiNG MOON

This is the phase when the moon is "shrinking." When you look up at the moon and the left side is what you see it is in the waning phase. This includes Waning Gibbous, Third Quarter (Half Moon), and Waning Crescent.

Release any negative patterns and beliefs that are holding you back. Examples: Release distractions that keep you from working with your guide like watching too much tv. Or, go on social media less to help you stay more positive about your life.

This is a good time to reflect on where you are with your intention. It is also an excellent time to declutter. Notice how you feel during this phase. Note what you are releasing on your bonus worksheet.

As you come to the next new moon, you can adjust your original intention or set a new intention. Be sure to thank yourself for your efforts. The end of this phase, before the next new moon, is sometimes called the Dark or Balsamic Moon. A perfect time to do some deep healing or simply rest.

Moving Forward

Woohoo! Go you! I hope this has been a beautiful journey.

This is not the end. This is the beginning. Free Spirit Living.

Enjoy this beautiful toolbox filled with fun and playful techniques to get you out of funks, create your dream life, tap into your energy field, and so on.

Refer back to it frequently.

For more Free Spirit Living Tips, please join my newsletter at www.kerryburki.com.

From one free spirit to another...xo. Thank you for being part of my world.

Love, Kerry

Bonuses

Be sure to check out all of the bonuses included with this guidebook:

- Printable Worksheets
- Guided Meditations
- Moving Forward - Planners and Ritual Sheets
- Working with your Printable Oracle Cards
- Moon Charting Lesson

www.kerryburki.com/free-spirit-bonuses

Bibliography & Recommended Reading

Melody Beattie: *Journey to the Heart*
Gabrielle Bernstein: *Miracles Now*
Claude M. Briston: *The Magic of Believing*
Sonia Choquette, *Trust Your Vibes*
Steven D. Farmer: *Animal Spirit Guides*
Louise Hay: *You Can Heal Your Life*
B.K.S. Iyengar: *Light On Yoga*
Guru Jagat: *Invincible Living*
Anodea Judith: *Chakras*
Goswami Kriyananda: *The Spiritual Science of Kriya Yoga*
Judith Lasater: *Living Your Yoga*
Philip Permutt: *The Crystal Healer*
Don Miguel Ruiz: *The Four Agreements*
Sivananda Yoga and Vedanta Center: *Yoga Mind & Body*
Tess Whitehurst: *Holistic Energy Magic, Good Energy, Magical Housekeeping*

www.kerryburki.com

Made in the USA
Lexington, KY
25 November 2019